The Bored STUPID at Work Doodle Book

THIS IS A CARLTON BOOK

This edition published in 2012 by Carlton Books
An imprint of the Carlton Publishing Group
20 Mortimer Street
London W1T 3JW

Images copyright © 2008 and 2009 Ross Adams
Design & layout copyright © 2012 Carlton Publishing Group

A CIP catalogue record for this book is available from the British Library

ISBN 978-1-84732-964-6

Printed in China

The images in this book were previously published in *The Bored@Work Doodle Book* & *The Really Bored@Work Doodle Book*

The Bored STUPID at Work Doodle Book

Escape your mind-numbing
drudgery with this scribble-in book

Rose Adders

CARLTON

Draw in this book

Colour in the images

Fill in the drawings

Stick things in it

Fill the pages with data

Cover the pages in something more
interesting

It's your book . . . use it!

Getting to know you

MY NAME IS:

BUT THEY CALL ME:

I WORK AS A:

FOR:

WITH:

I LIKE MY JOB BECAUSE:

I LOOK LIKE THIS:

MY FACE AT WORK:

MY FACE AFTER WORK:

I WANT TO GET BETTER AT:

Load your gun with highlighter ink and defend the office from hostile takeover

Rate your job satisfaction

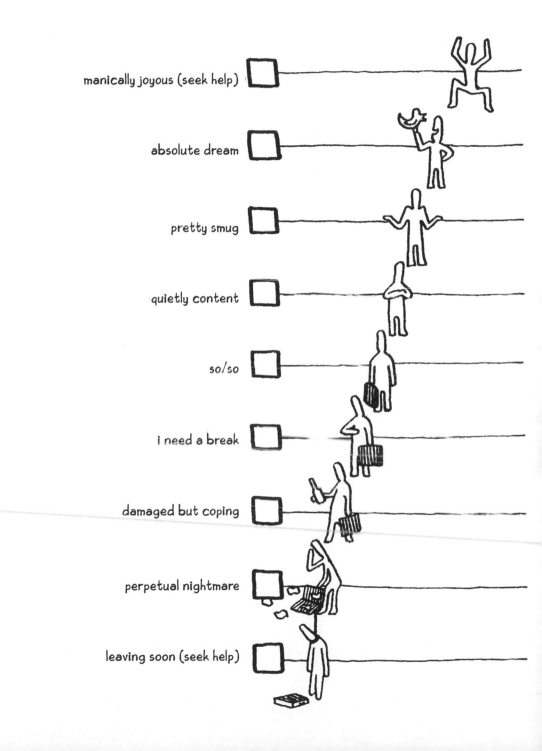

manically joyous (seek help) ☐

absolute dream ☐

pretty smug ☐

quietly content ☐

so/so ☐

i need a break ☐

damaged but coping ☐

perpetual nightmare ☐

leaving soon (seek help) ☐

What else can you sweep under the carpet?

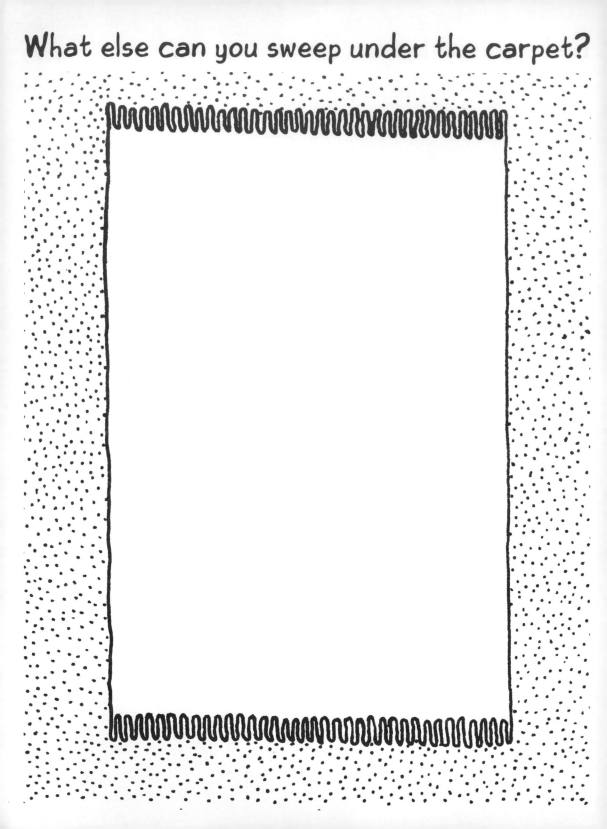

(At the end of the day...) Turn off the lights and leave...

Reinterpret the nearest piece of office art

Give these noses an appropriate colour

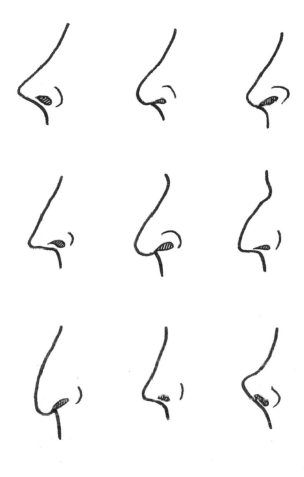

Career snakes and ladders

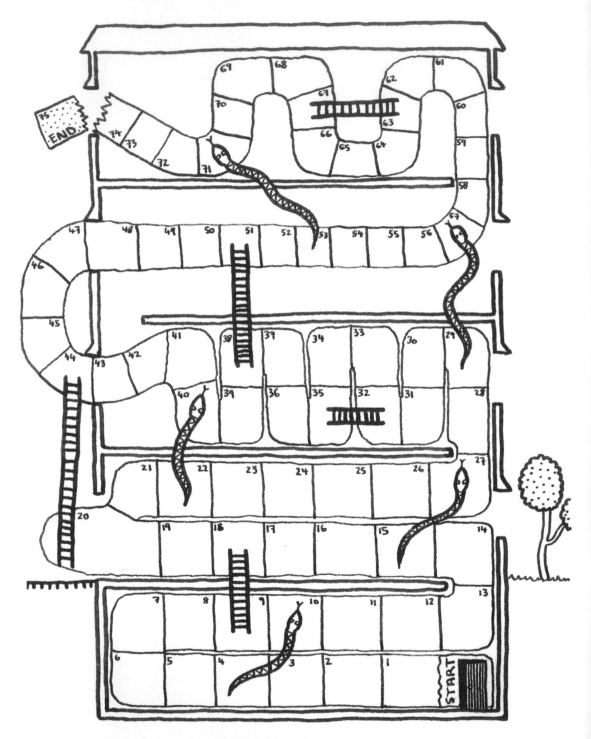

Start a fire and evacuate everyone

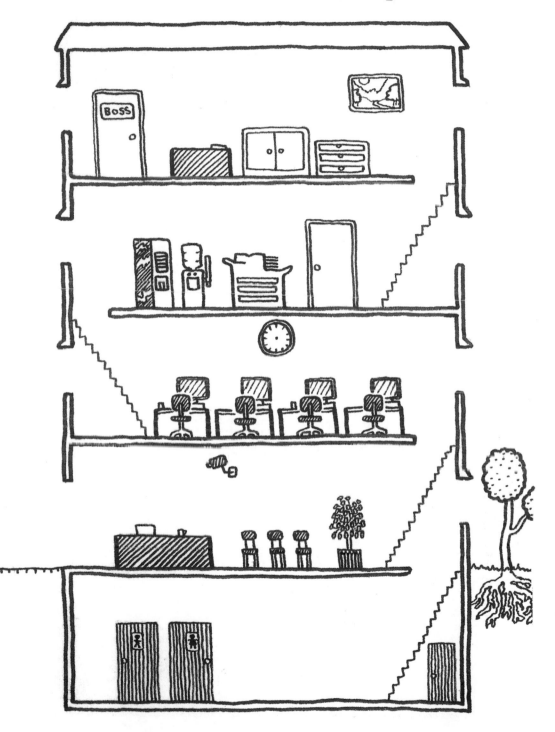

How full is your cup?

bottomless (seek help)

brimming

plenty left

couple of gulps

realistic - mid-range

few sips

dregs

kettle on

what cup? (seek help)

Draw some more interesting learning curves

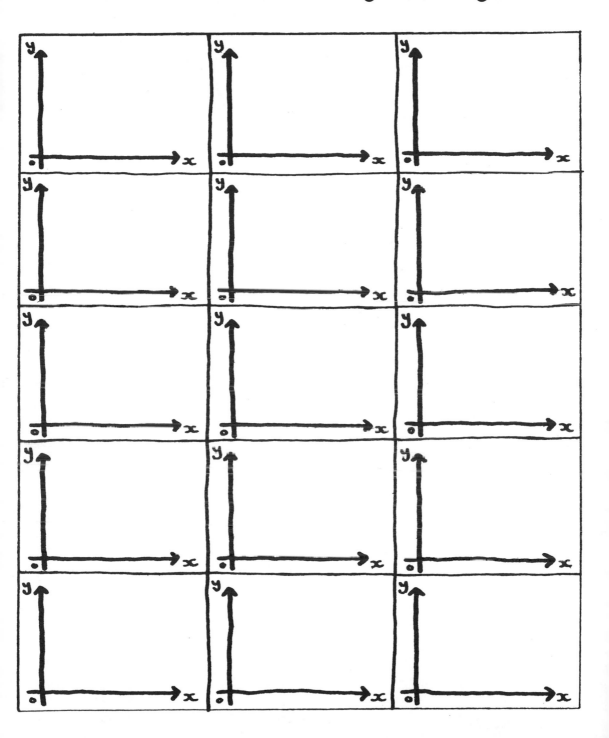

Dress your co-workers for the weekend

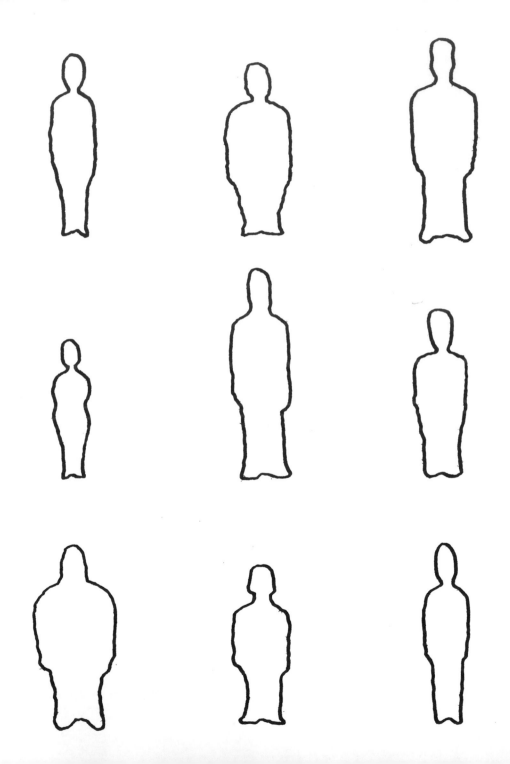

Write the inside of your own leaving card

*Sorry to hear
that you are leaving.*

Draw the team dogsbodies

Make a mug-ring galaxy

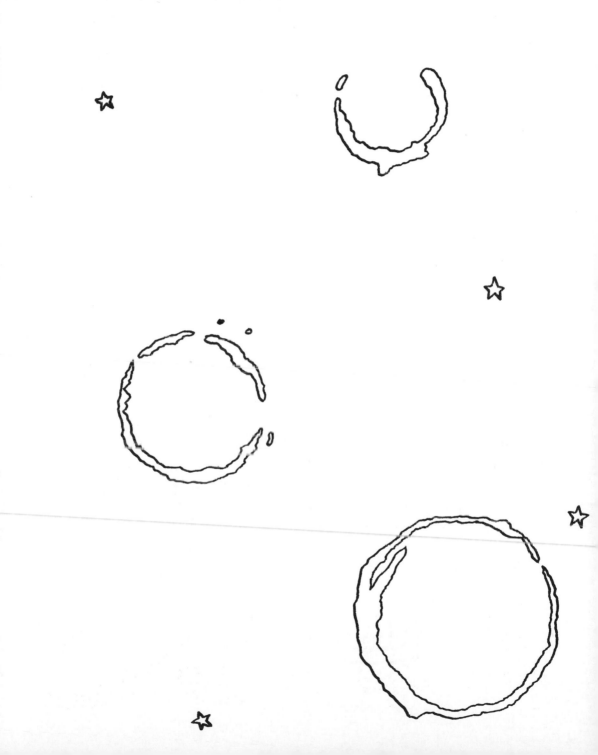

Do some proper cherry picking

Award three points for first place, two for second and one for third

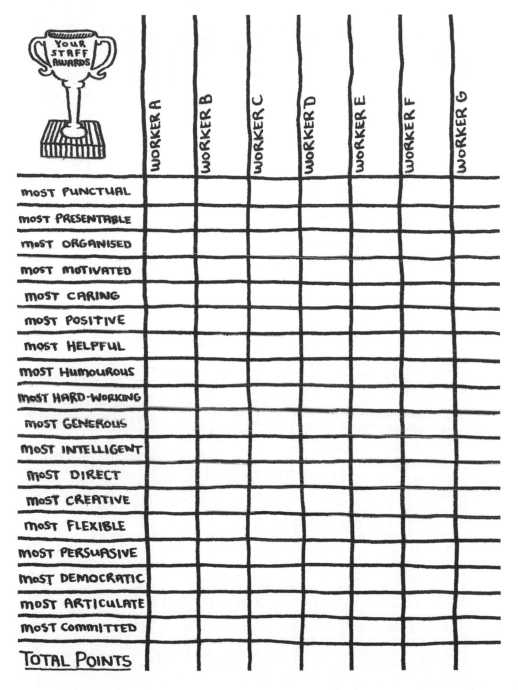

YOUR STAFF AWARDS	WORKER A	WORKER B	WORKER C	WORKER D	WORKER E	WORKER F	WORKER G
MOST PUNCTUAL							
MOST PRESENTABLE							
MOST ORGANISED							
MOST MOTIVATED							
MOST CARING							
MOST POSITIVE							
MOST HELPFUL							
MOST HUMOUROUS							
MOST HARD-WORKING							
MOST GENEROUS							
MOST INTELLIGENT							
MOST DIRECT							
MOST CREATIVE							
MOST FLEXIBLE							
MOST PERSUASIVE							
MOST DEMOCRATIC							
MOST ARTICULATE							
MOST COMMITTED							
TOTAL POINTS							

Executive decision maker: close your eyes and let your pen guide you

Make your own money

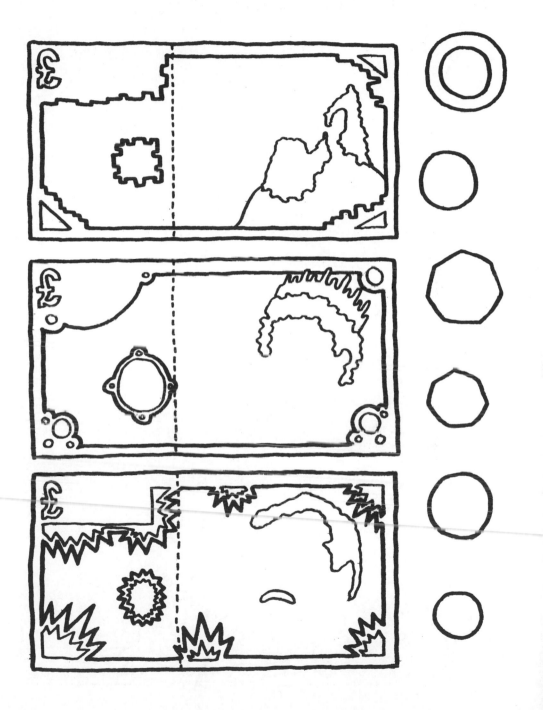

Fill in your expanding job description balloon

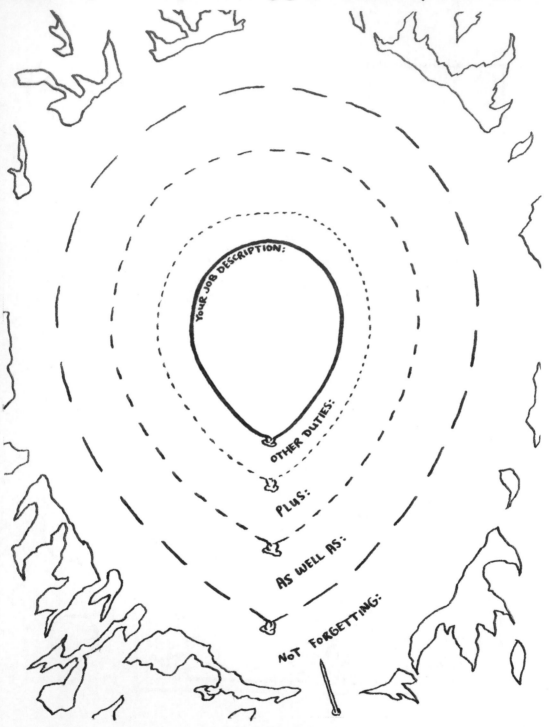

YOUR JOB DESCRIPTION:

OTHER DUTIES:

PLUS:

AS WELL AS:

NOT FORGETTING:

See your week in pies: one slice = one hour

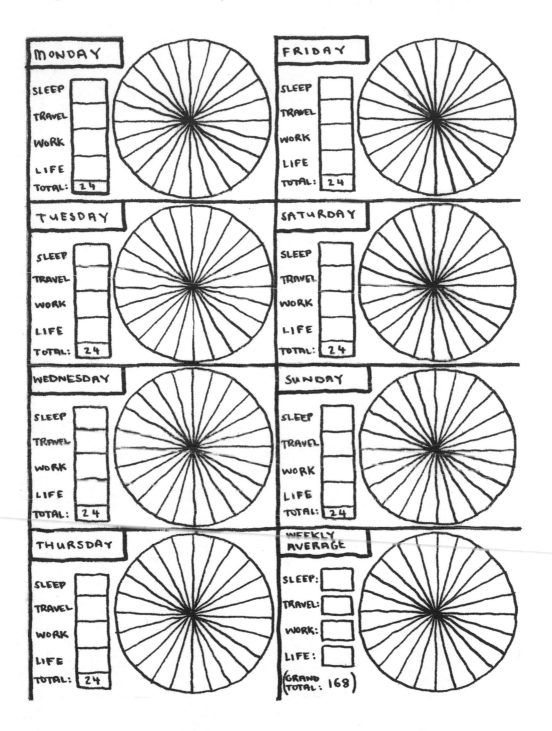

MONDAY

SLEEP
TRAVEL
WORK
LIFE
TOTAL: 24

FRIDAY

SLEEP
TRAVEL
WORK
LIFE
TOTAL: 24

TUESDAY

SLEEP
TRAVEL
WORK
LIFE
TOTAL: 24

SATURDAY

SLEEP
TRAVEL
WORK
LIFE
TOTAL: 24

WEDNESDAY

SLEEP
TRAVEL
WORK
LIFE
TOTAL: 24

SUNDAY

SLEEP
TRAVEL
WORK
LIFE
TOTAL: 24

THURSDAY

SLEEP
TRAVEL
WORK
LIFE
TOTAL: 24

WEEKLY
AVERAGE

SLEEP:
TRAVEL:
WORK:
LIFE:

(GRAND
TOTAL: 168)

Brainstorm on this page

Design a fortnight of wacky ties

week 1:

week 2:

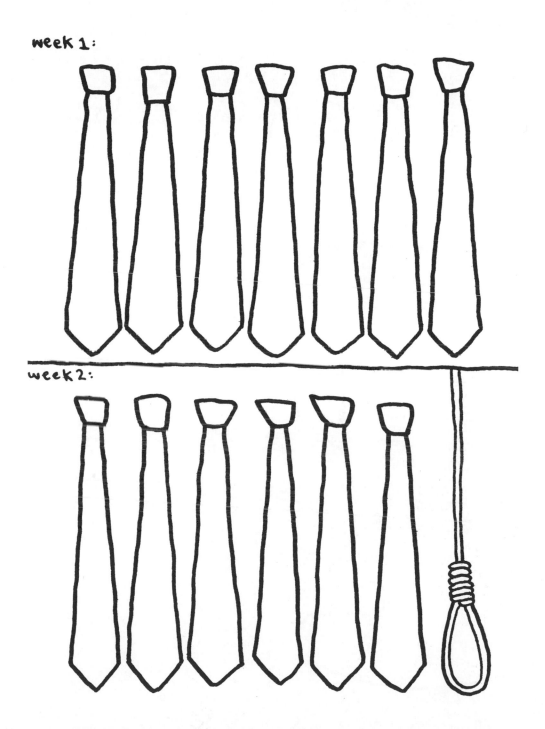

What's left after you have liquidated all your assets?

Who won the rat race?

OMG who's lunchbox is this?

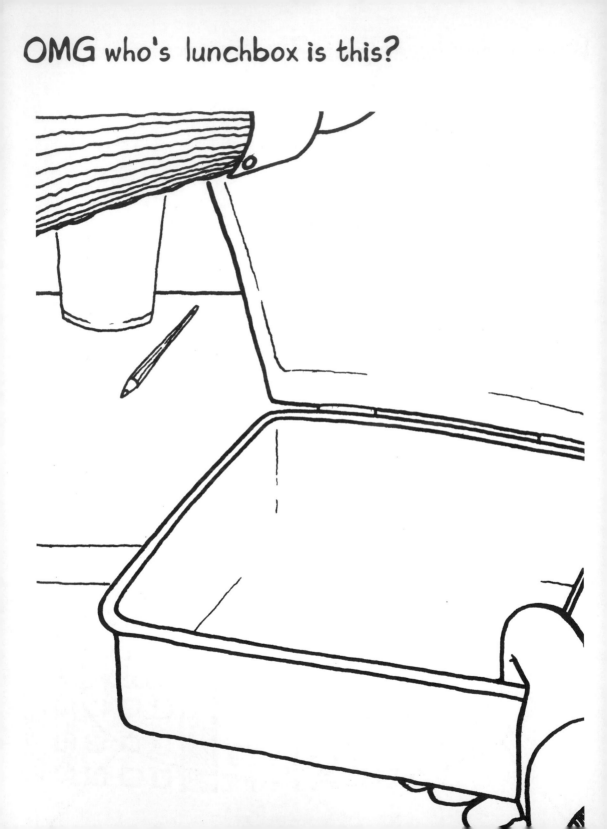

Draw some bubbles in the watercooler

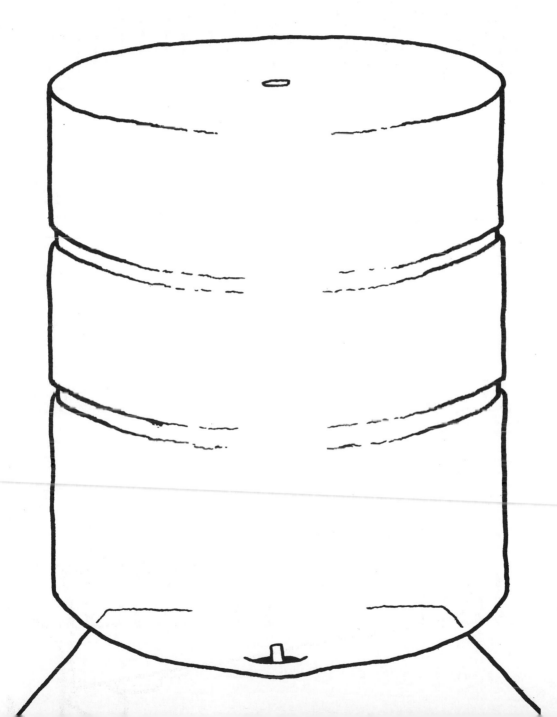

Add some bullet points

Voodoo co-workers - do your worst

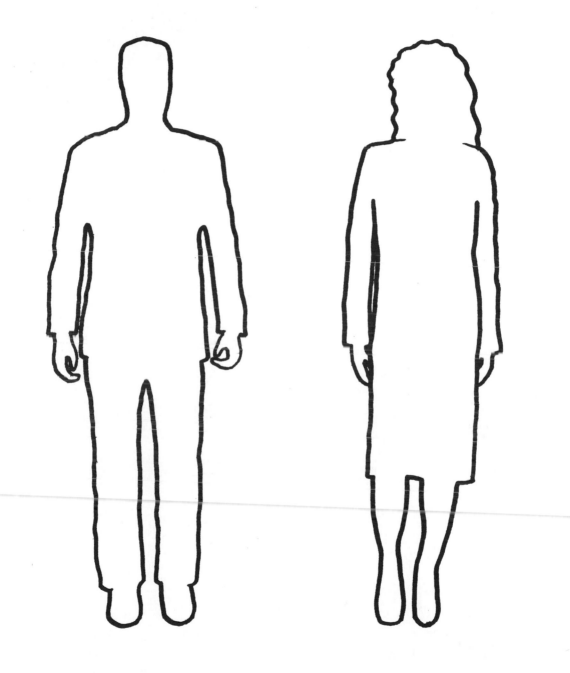

What is rolling downhill?

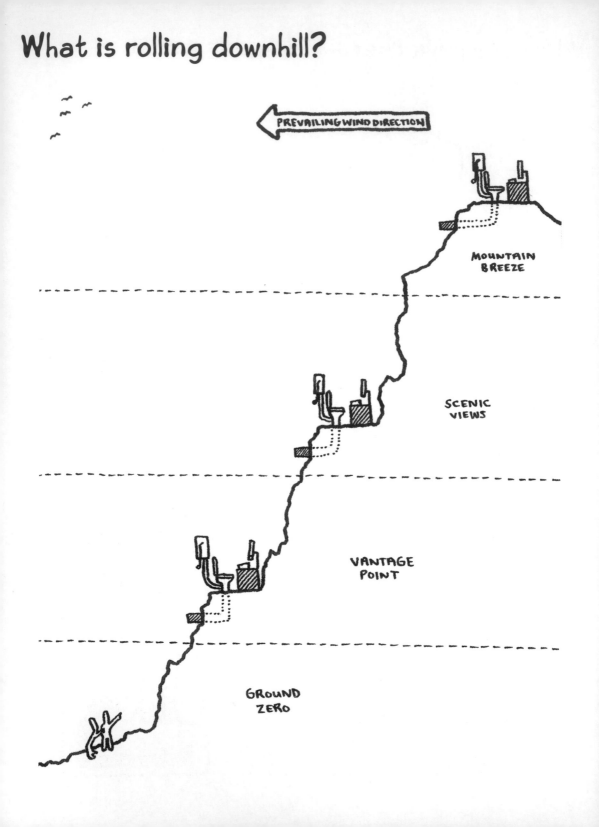

Fill the team's trophy cabinet

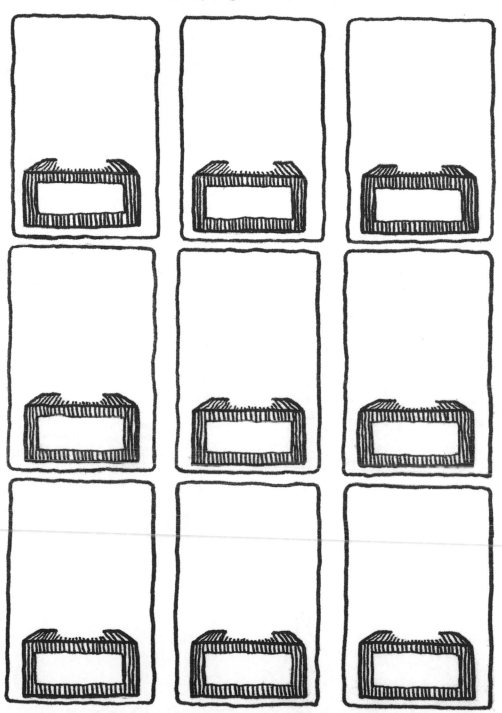

What thoughts are really outside the box?

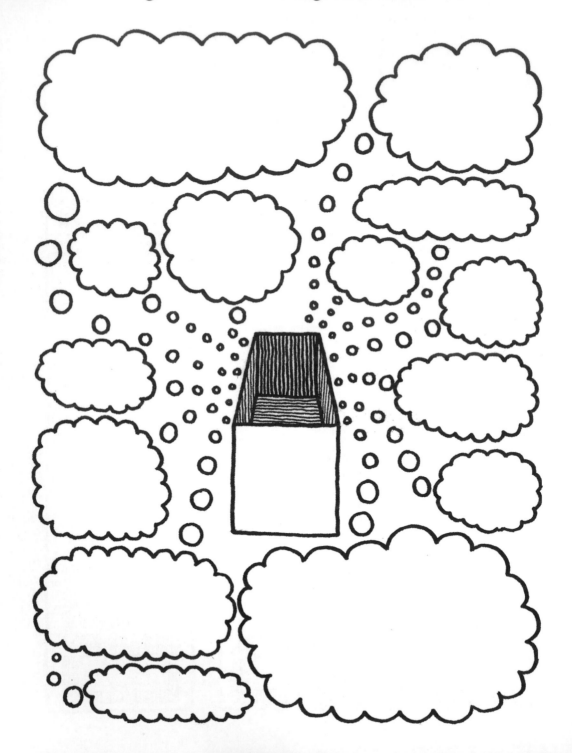

Draw in the middleman

What messages would you like to get?

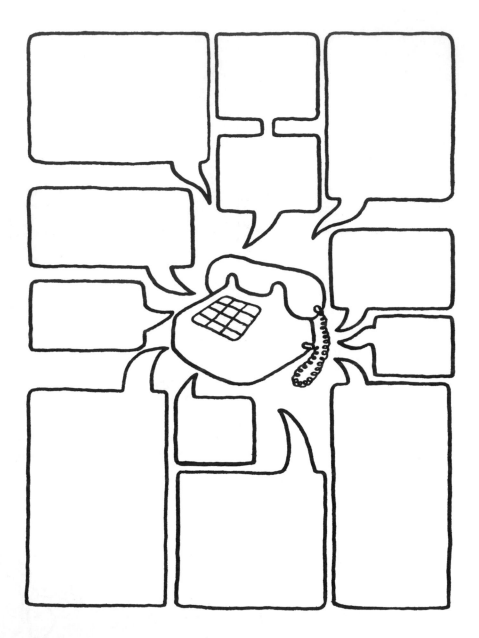

Cut-out-and-keep Carriage Clock

Bail your team out . . . but mind what they land on

Design more bugs for your computer

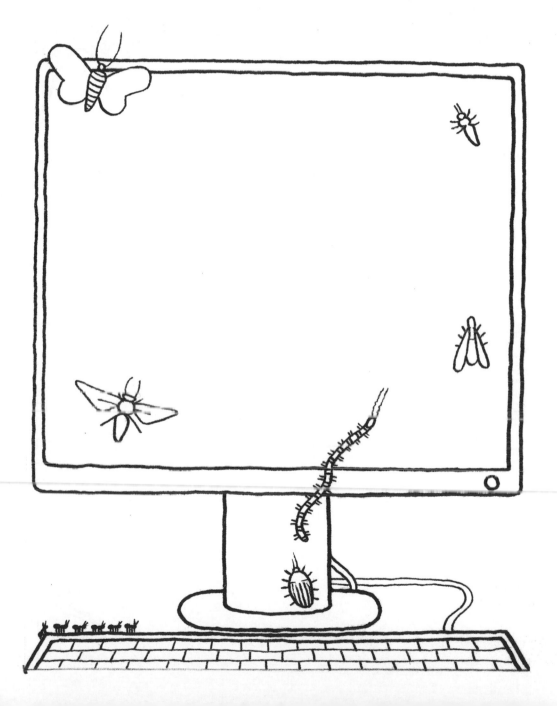

Whats at the end of the line you are towing?

Lace up and reboot your computer

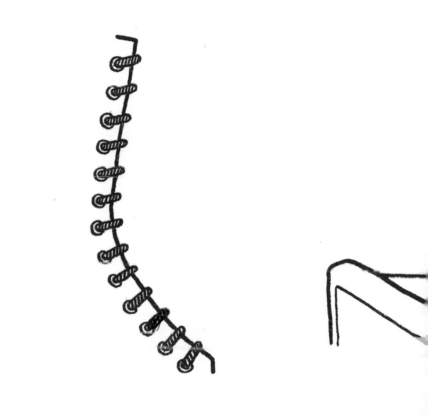

Draw as many health and safety violations as possible

Junk mail wall of fame

Draw your ultimate office party

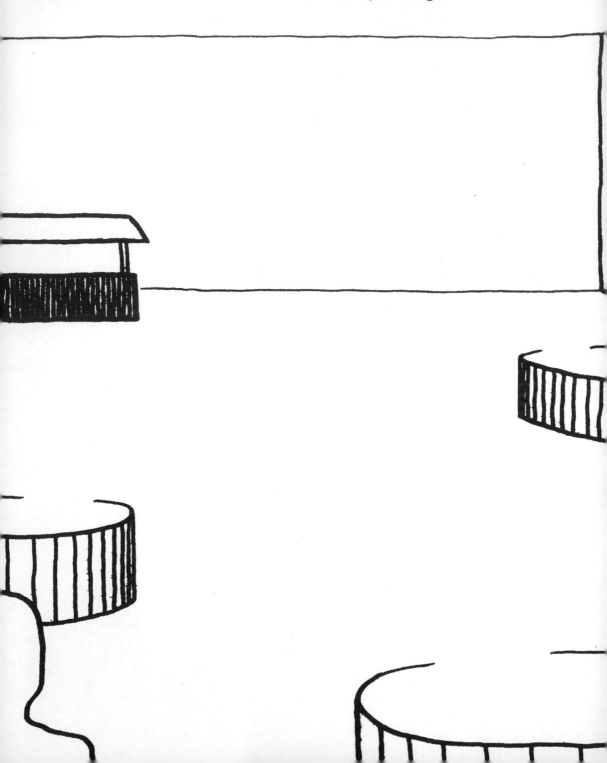

What's stopping you from getting the sack?

Lay your big idea on the table

What happens when you get fired?

Who would you employ? complete each applicant's picture and tick to accept them

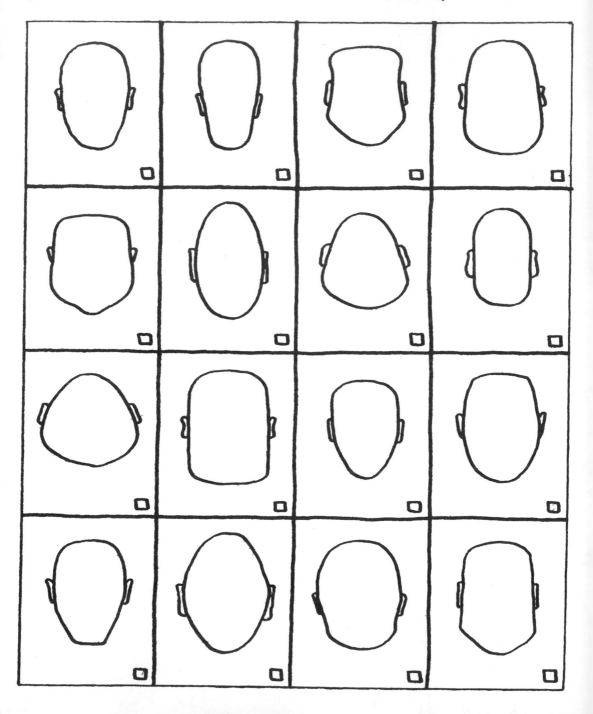

Draw what you can see out of the nearest office window

What does your slice of the cake look like?

It's rush hour: how many bodies can you cram in each mode of transport?

Draw what you would like to see out of the nearest office window

Rate your enjoyment of each day and plot your Happy Graph

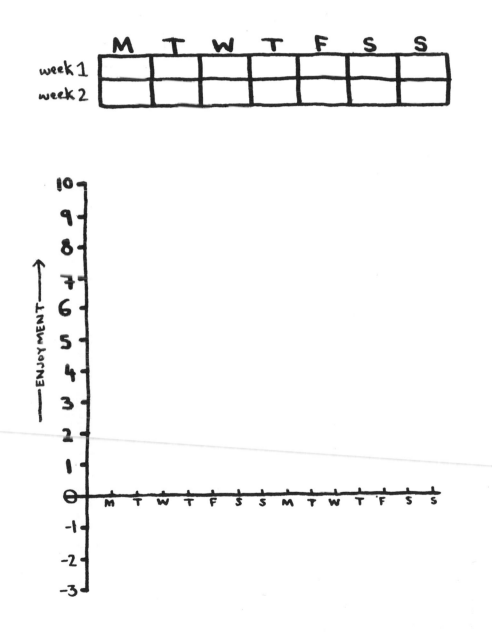

Make both ends meet

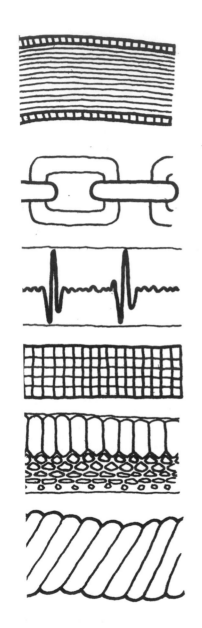

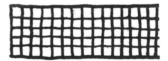
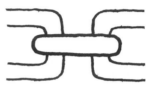
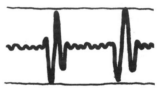
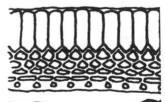

Complete the detail on these biscuits

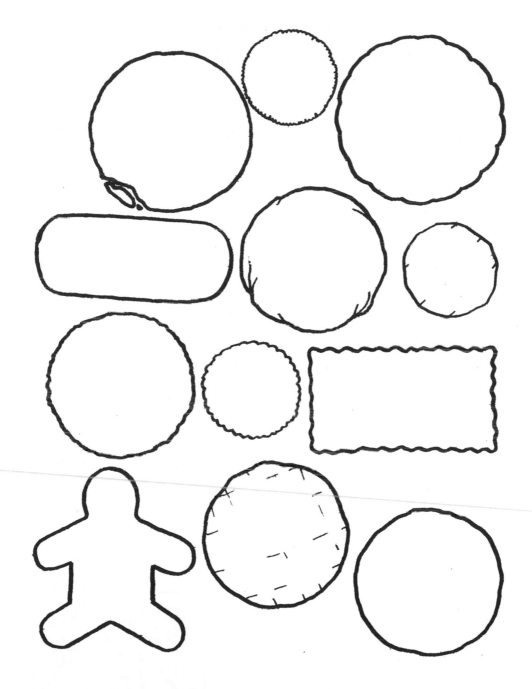

Mark off each day on your prison wall year planner

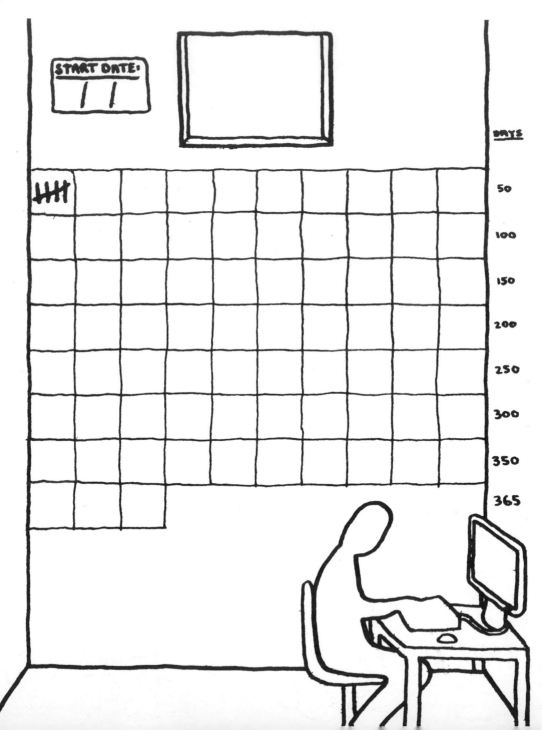

Are the mice eating the big cheese?

Please complete the bored @ work diagnosis sheet

- **DATA COMA** (i am in a) ☐
- **DUVET COMMITMENTS** (i have periodic) ☐
- **OBJECT MISUSE** (regular patterns of) ☐
- **NUTRITION DIVERSIONS** (i take) ☐
- **TELEPHONIC ALLERGIES** (i experience) ☐
- **STRESS FRACTURES** (i have multiple) ☐
- **BOTTOMLESS INBOX** (i have a) ☐
- **MALIGNANT MANAGEMENT** (a case of) ☐
- **KEYBOARD BOXING** (i train in) ☐
- **CONCENTRATION LAPSE** (....look! a pen!) ☐
- **FOGHORN THROAT** (i suffer from) ☐
- **GHOST TEAM** (i am surrounded by a) ☐
- **TECHNICAL HITCHES** (i am covered in) ☐
- **EXPECTATION CEILING** (i have reached my) ☐
- **PRINTER MAGNETISM** (i have daily) ☐
- **OPTION PARALYSIS** (i have) ☐
- **"UNOFFICIAL RESEARCH"** (i conduct) ☐
- **FLAPPING MOUTH** (i have bouts of) ☐
- **WINDOW FIXATING** (i find myself) ☐
- **OVERWORKED** (i am) ☐
- **UNDERPAID** (i am) ☐

Which automated device is Dave caught in?

What's happened to Dave?

Groundhog Day: make each day different

What would happen if the cleaner didn't come in for a year?

You decide what is on each floor

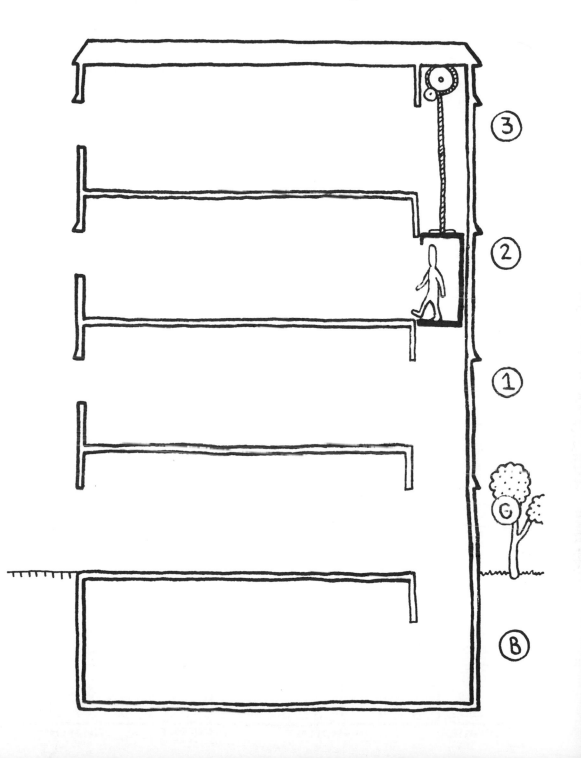

Complete the cycle of illness

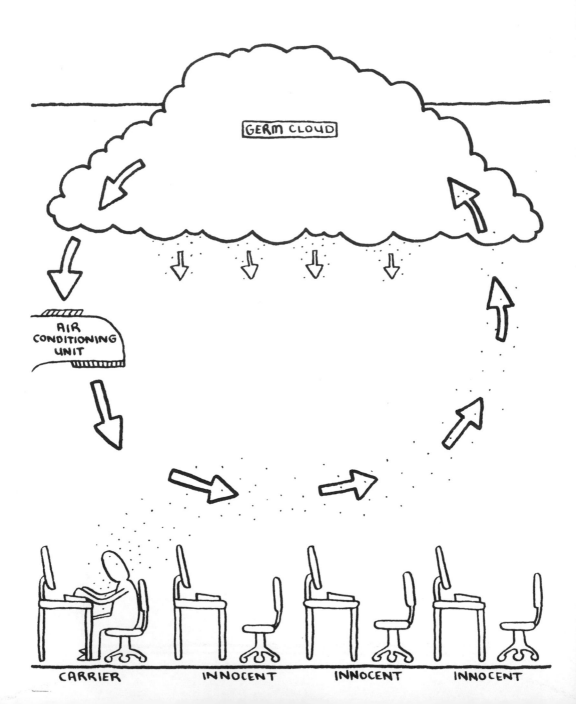

Make a chessboard on the ceiling tiles

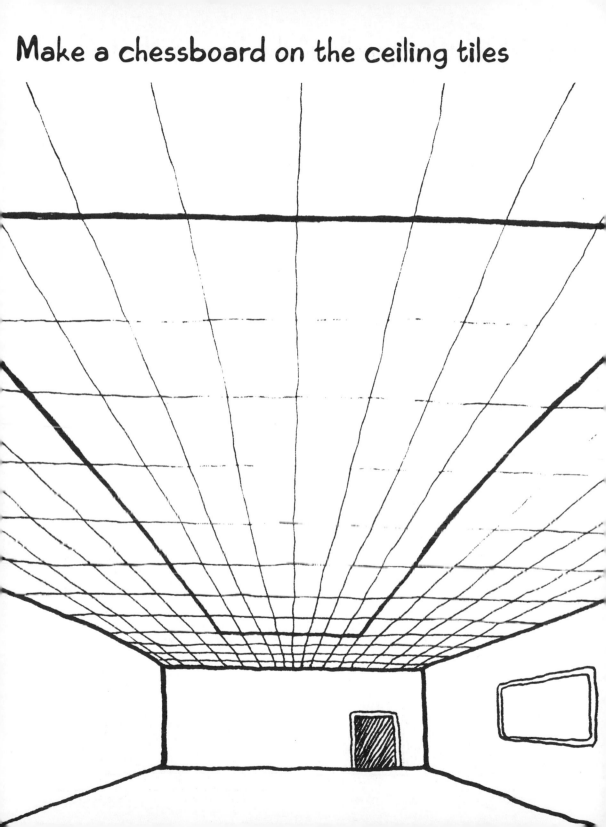

Who's in charge of all the honey that the worker bees have made?

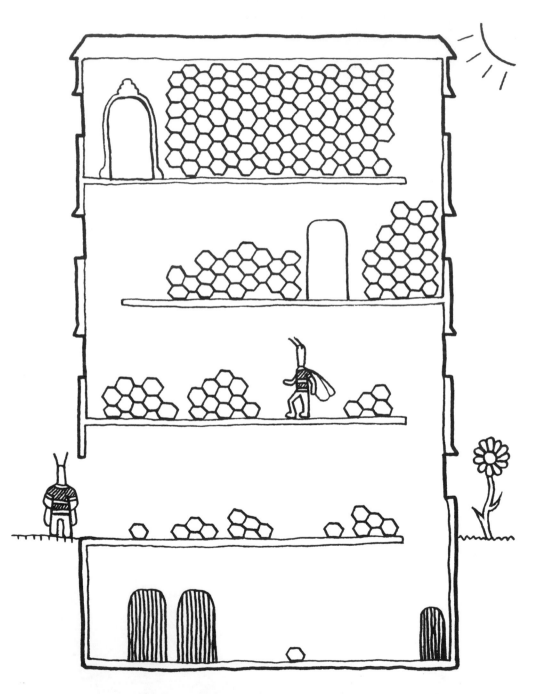

Defend your desk from invasion

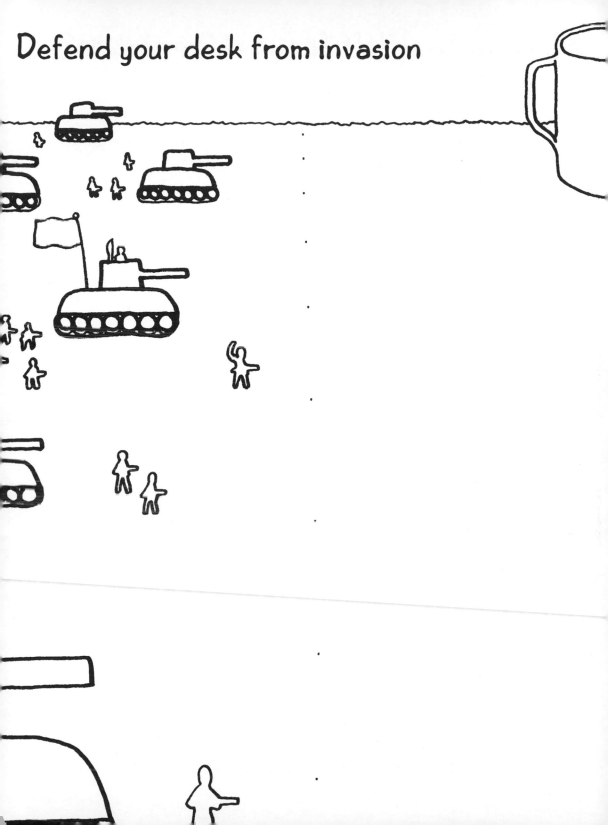

What has been left for you in reception?

Accountability: point the finger of blame

Who made your printer jam?

Keep yourself busy — fill your in and out trays

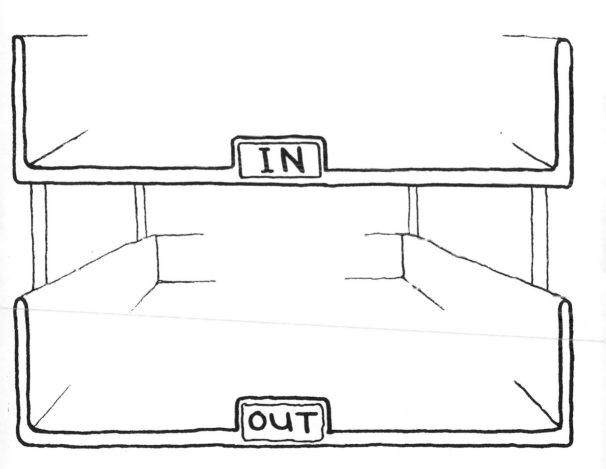

What grows in the office?

Go with the flow

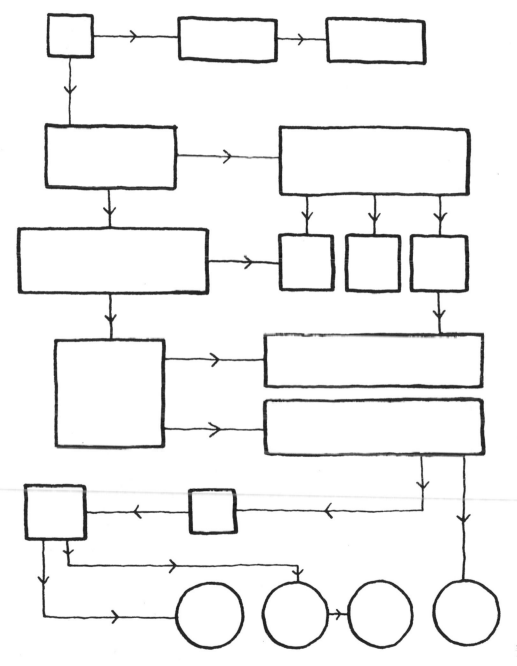

Paint your nails

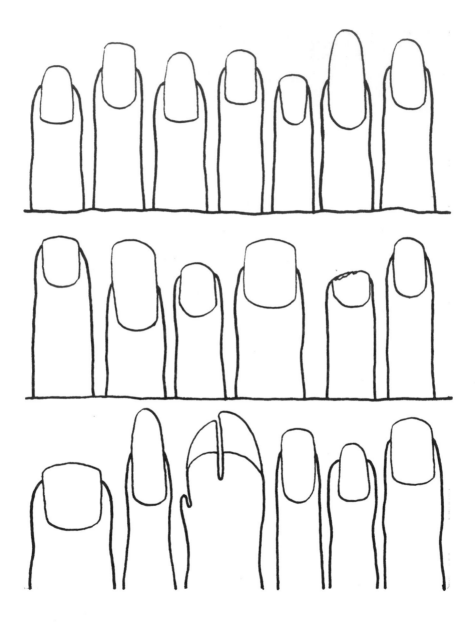

Give your resignation presentation

Add some rungs to the career ladders

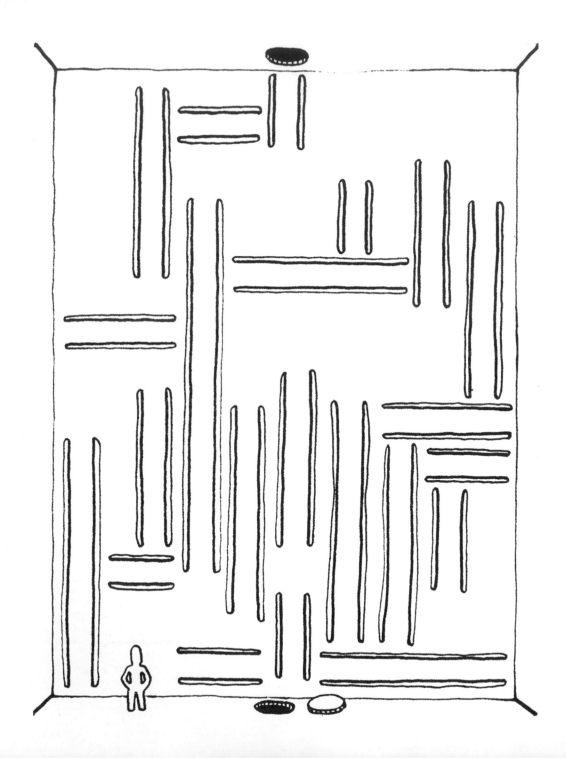

How do you look after number one?

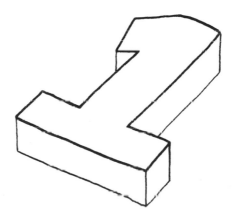

Avoid the bulls___, brand the cashcows and escape on the gravy train

Your notes

Do your own photocopying!

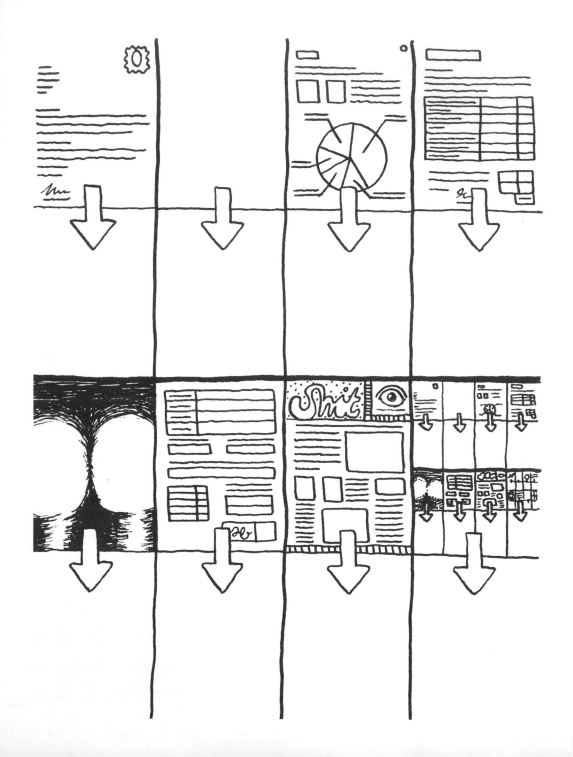

How can you adapt to the desk job?

Who exactly is in the same boat as you?
Where is everyone else?

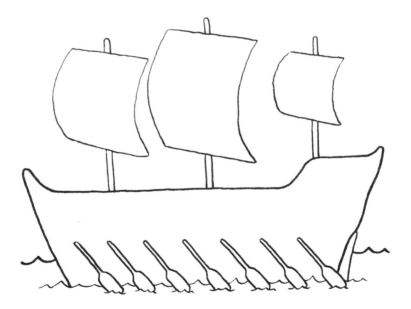

What's inside the work bags, and who do they belong to?

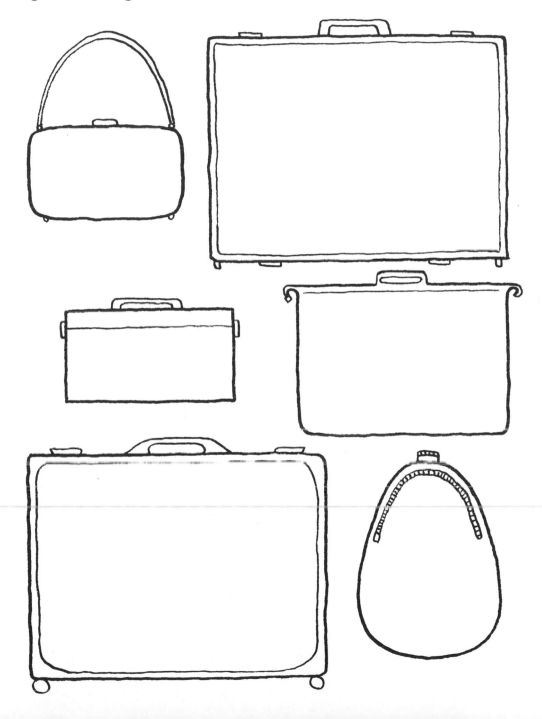

Are all your cheques in the post?

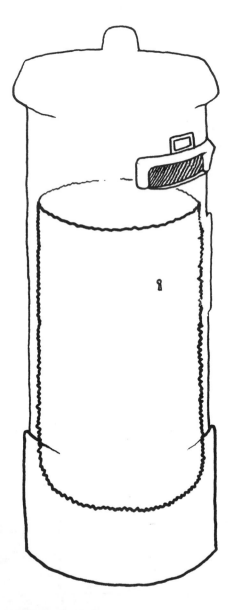

Draw your own motivational poster

SUCCESS

Discredit your colleague,
and you will shine.

Know the competition/know yourself

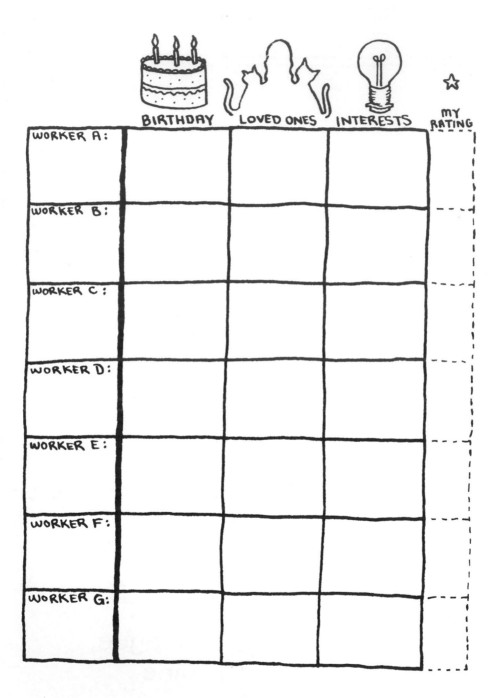

	BIRTHDAY	LOVED ONES	INTERESTS	MY RATING
WORKER A:				
WORKER B:				
WORKER C:				
WORKER D:				
WORKER E:				
WORKER F:				
WORKER G:				

What can you see in the chad storm?

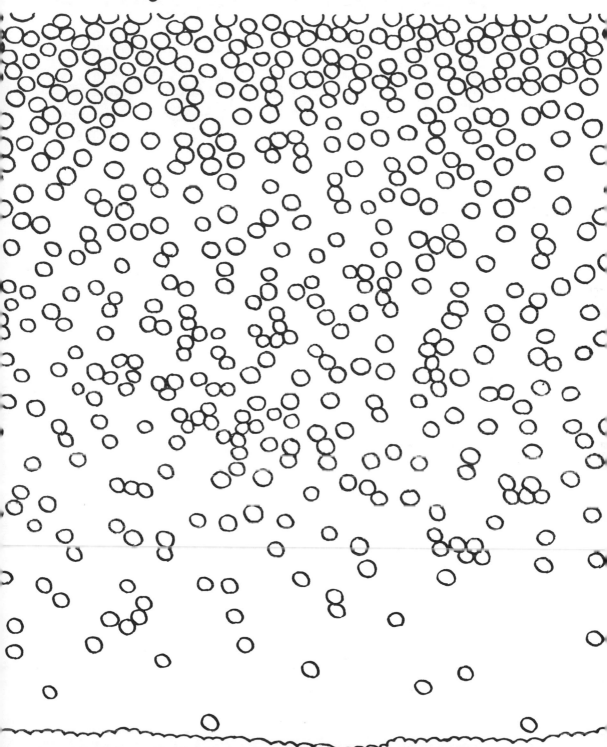

Who has been shipwrecked?

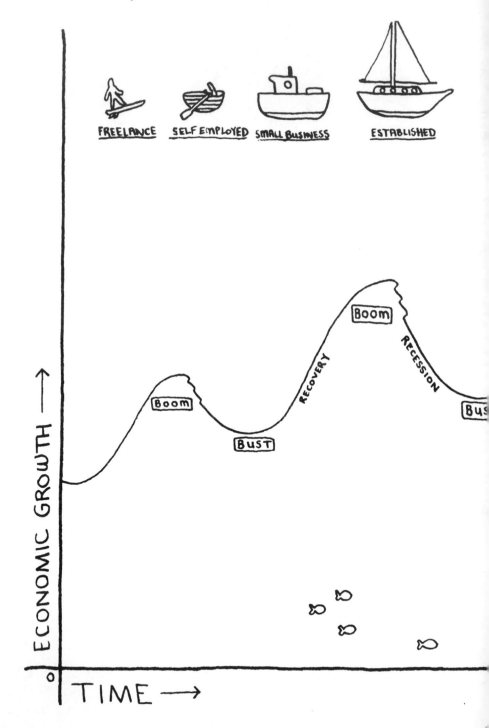

BIG BUSINESS

CORPORATE

SOLO

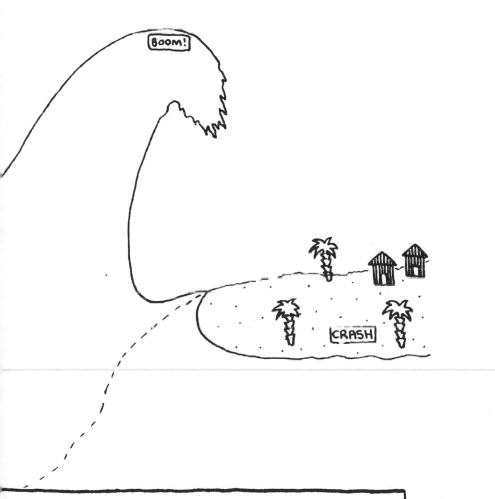

BOOM!

CRASH

Make these workers tear their hair out

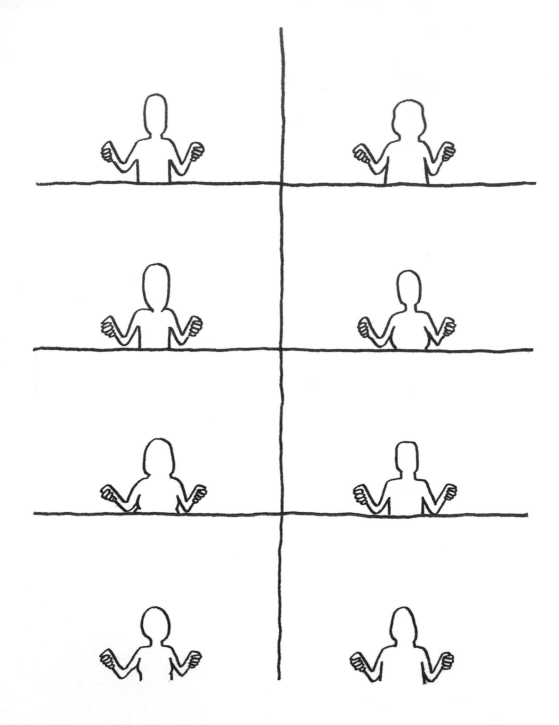

Add to these office viewpoints
(corridor, desk, keyboard, clock)

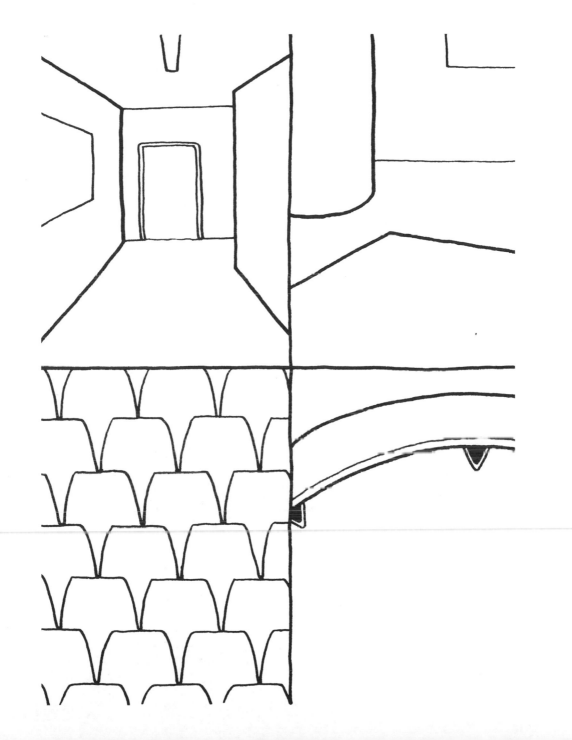

Where are you in the field of employment?

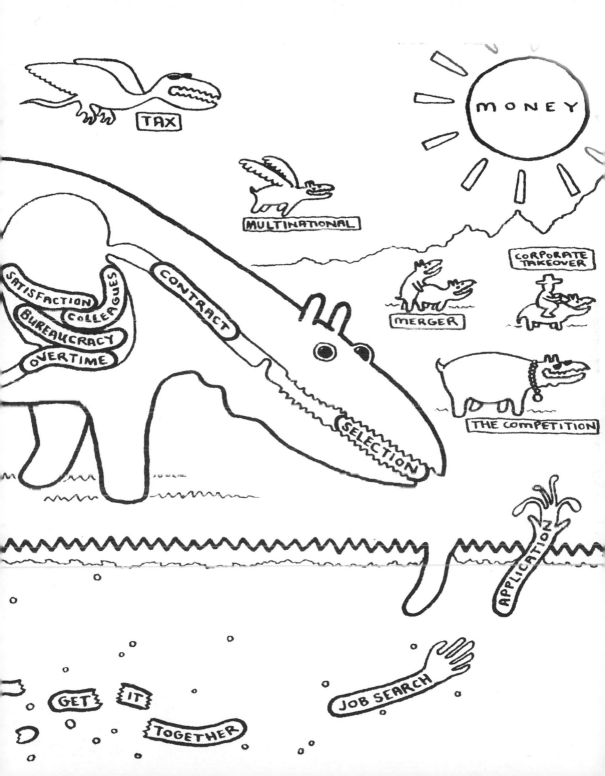

Frank the mail.

You don't have to be a

To work here,
But it helps.

Complete the 12-step Workaholics Program

① SURRENDER THE PROBLEM   ② CALM DOWN

③ SUBMIT TOTALLY   ④ SELF ANALYSE

⑤ IDENTIFY PERSONAL GOALS   ⑥ FLOOR THE HARDRIVE

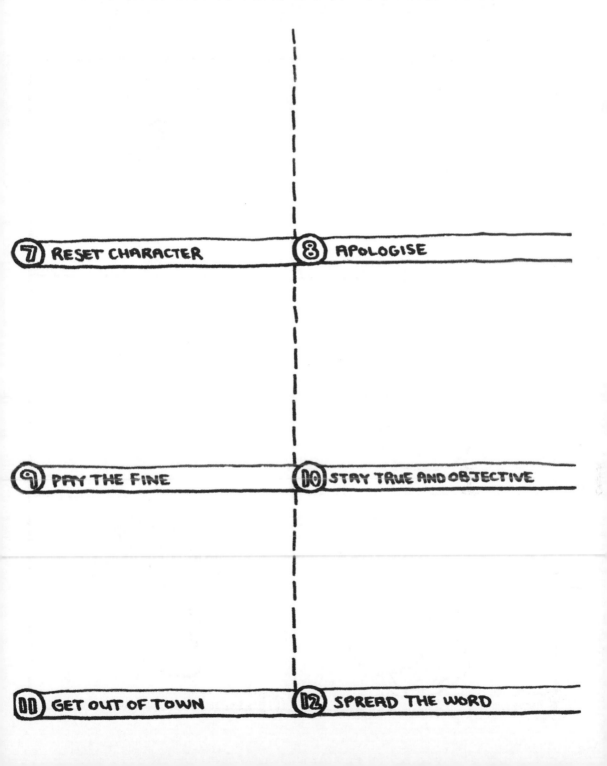

Does your mouse have a life of its own?

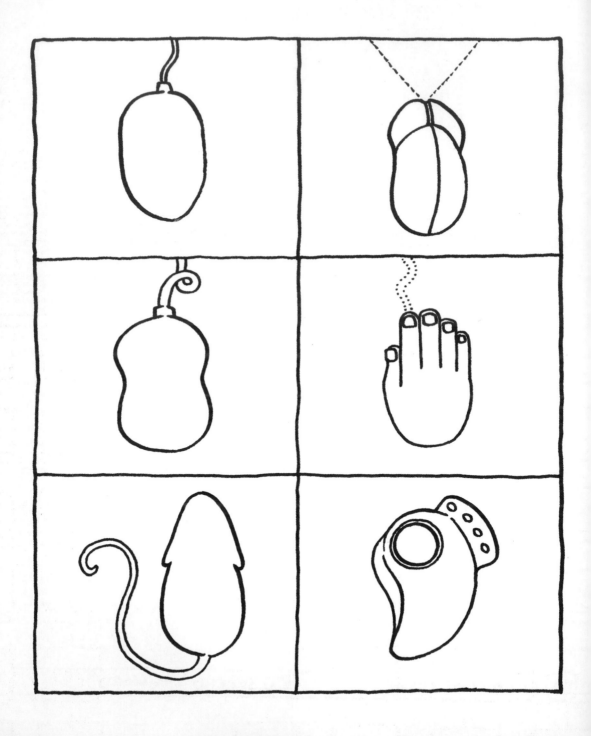

Climb the middle management skyscraper- but don't fall between jobs.

What is really going on inside your computer?

What is on the keyboards?

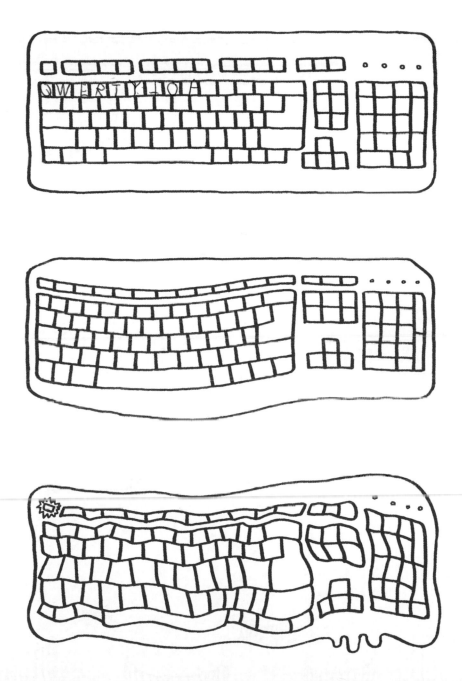

Sort out the paper problem.

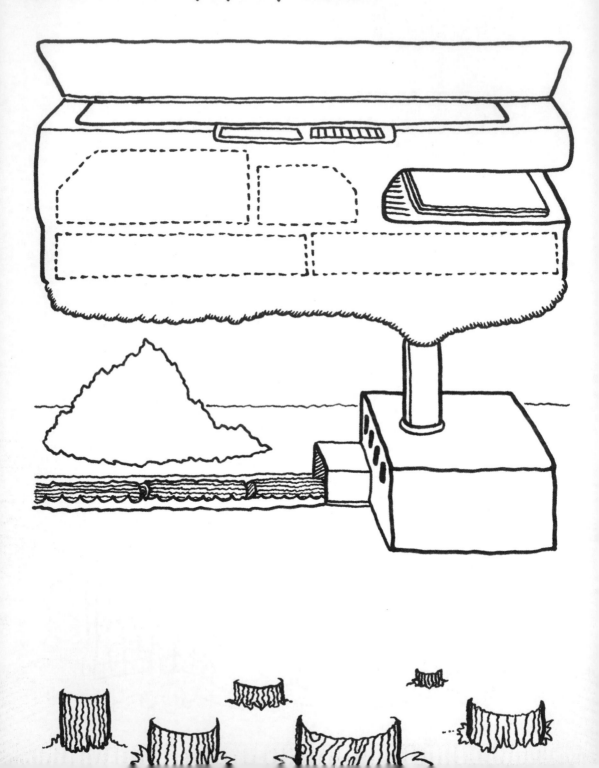

What would you like to see on your desk first thing on Monday morning?

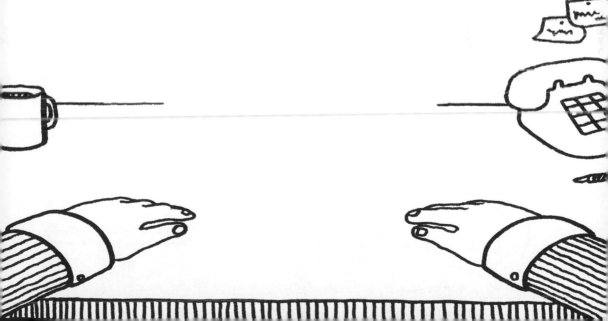

Rebrand the company logos.

Complete the control panel for the robot that will take over your job.

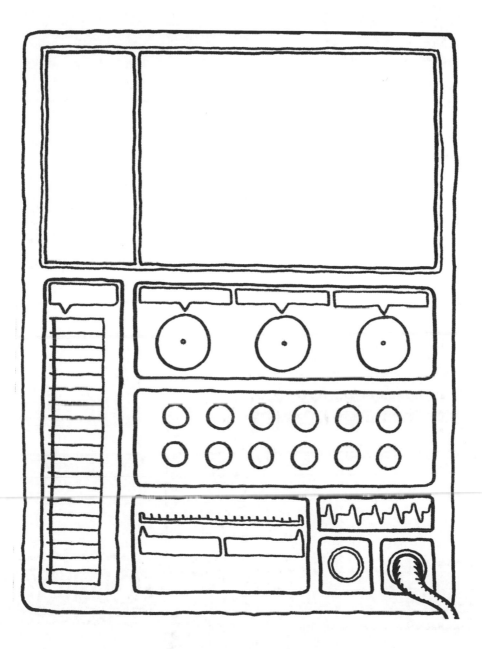

Job hunting? Sell yourself.

NEW

YOUR NAME HERE:

YOUR UNIQUE SELLING POINT:

YOUR EYE-CATCHING IMAGE:

NOW WITH MORE

YOUR IMPROVED FEATURES:

PLUS

ONLY

£ PER ANNUM

Try out the new pencil sharpener.

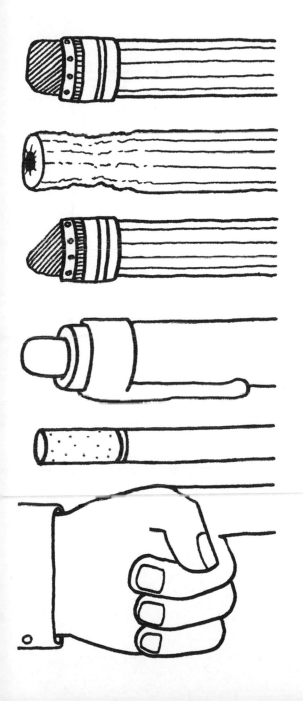

Send a Trojan Horse into the shared drive.

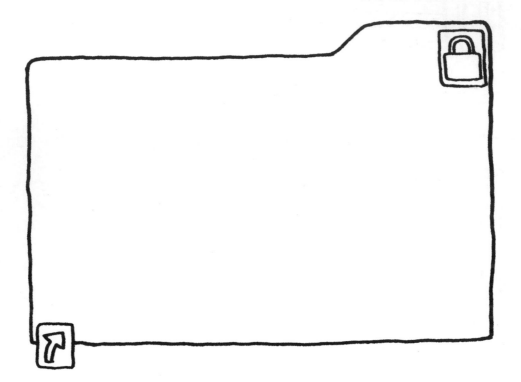

Will you survive re-entry into the work atmosphere as you return from your travels?

Who would you like to put on the coconut shy?

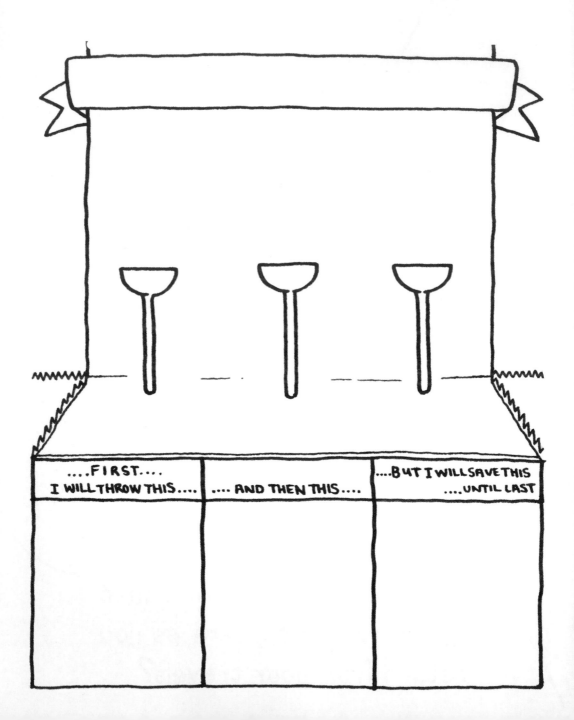

....FIRST....
I WILL THROW THIS....

.... AND THEN THIS....

....BUT I WILL SAVE THIS
....UNTIL LAST

Read your career future in the cappucino froth.

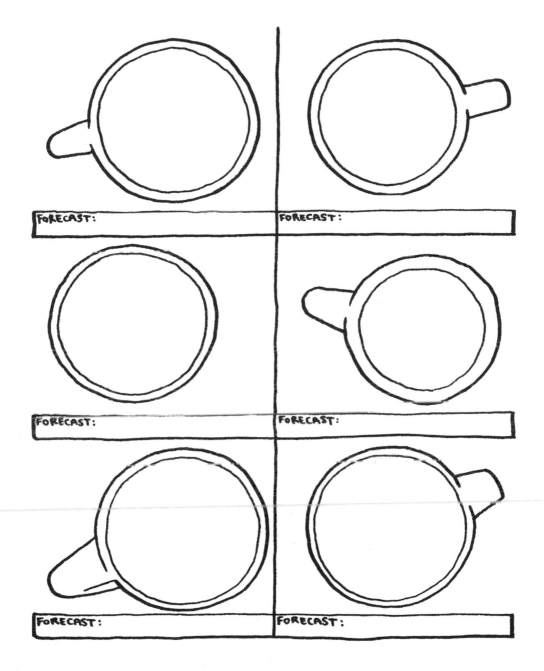

FORECAST:

FORECAST:

FORECAST:

FORECAST:

FORECAST:

FORECAST:

Draw yourself getting snapped up by the big fish or the loan shark.

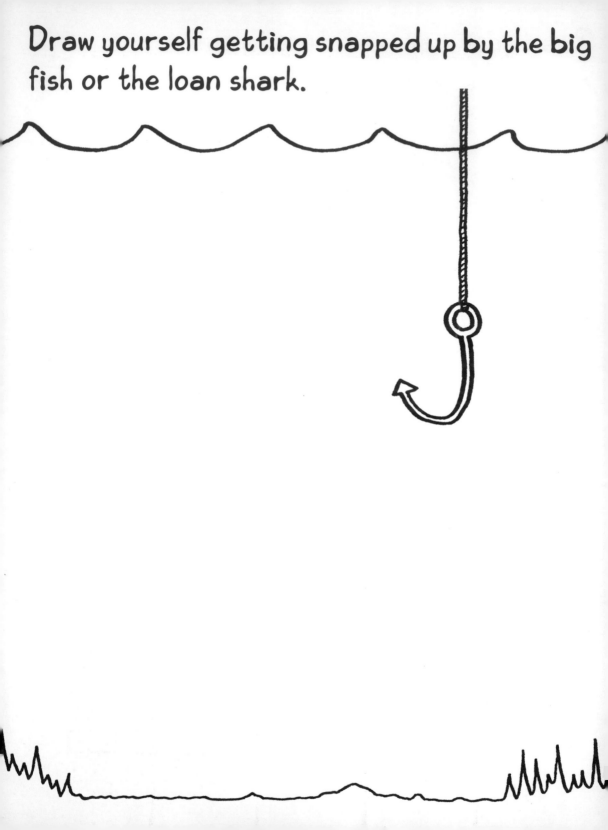

Bend these paperclips into new shapes or useful tools.

Use this page to help you follow those epic meetings.

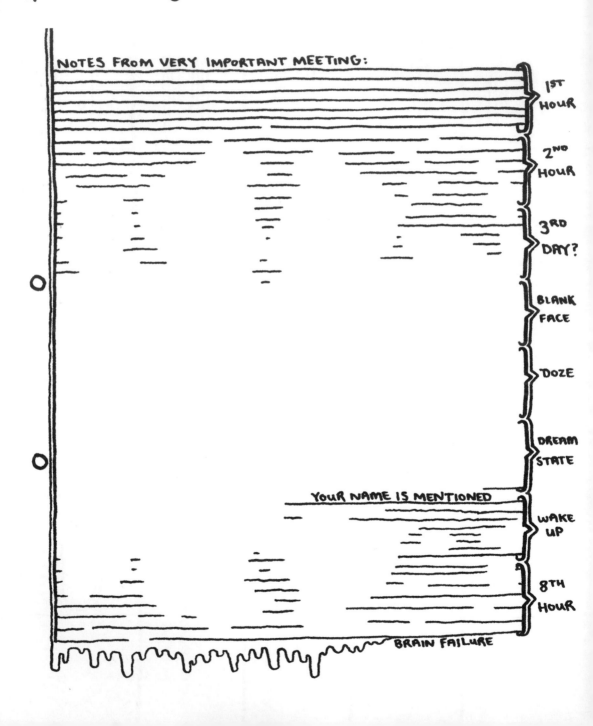

Finish off your colleagues' notes.

Uh-oh. What did you have to rescue from the paper shredder?

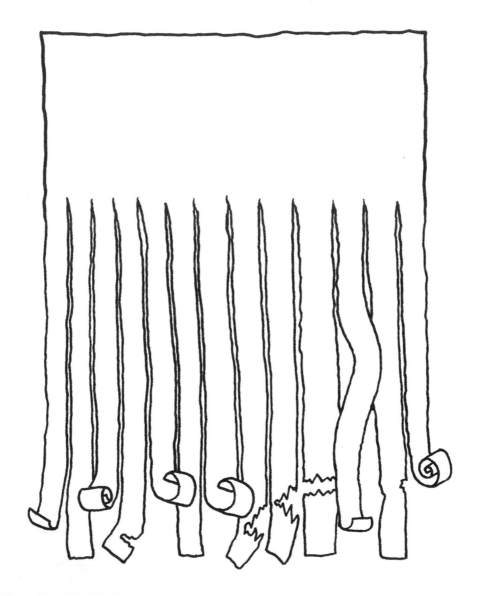

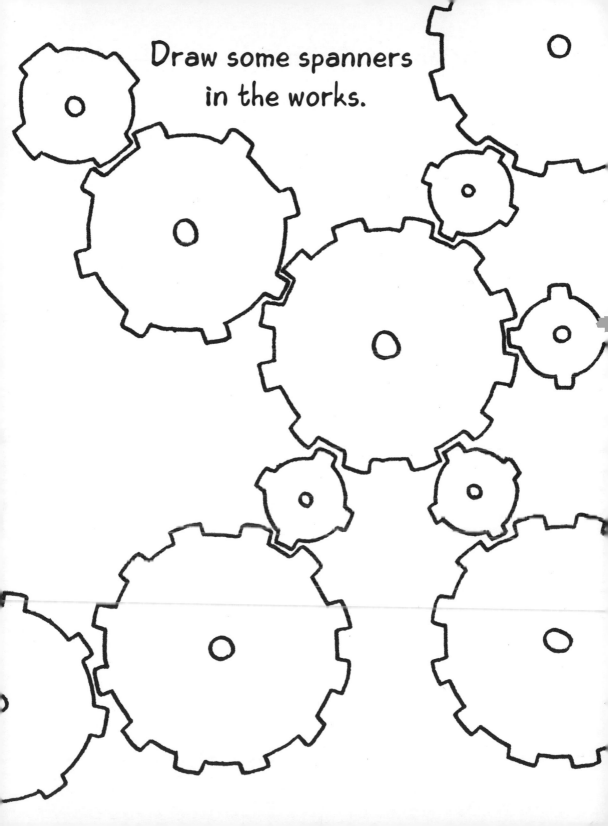

Draw some spanners
in the works.

Launch some new branches.

Save energy... and paint the bulbs black.

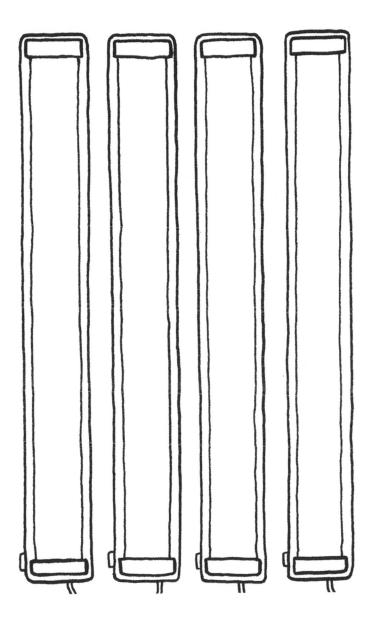

Write your own interview.

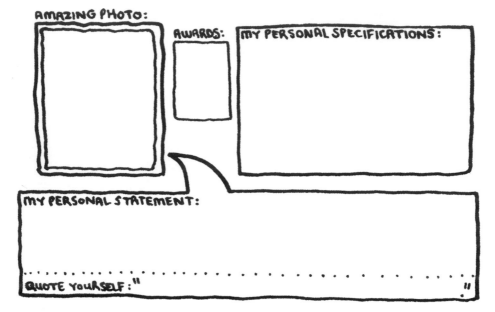

AMAZING PHOTO:

AWARDS:

MY PERSONAL SPECIFICATIONS:

MY PERSONAL STATEMENT:

QUOTE YOURSELF: "   "

ASK ME THESE QUESTIONS:	MY ANSWERS ARE:

YOU SHOULD EMPLOY ME BECAUSE:

Design your own Credit Crunch cereal and eat it for breakfast!

Who is still on the sinking ship?

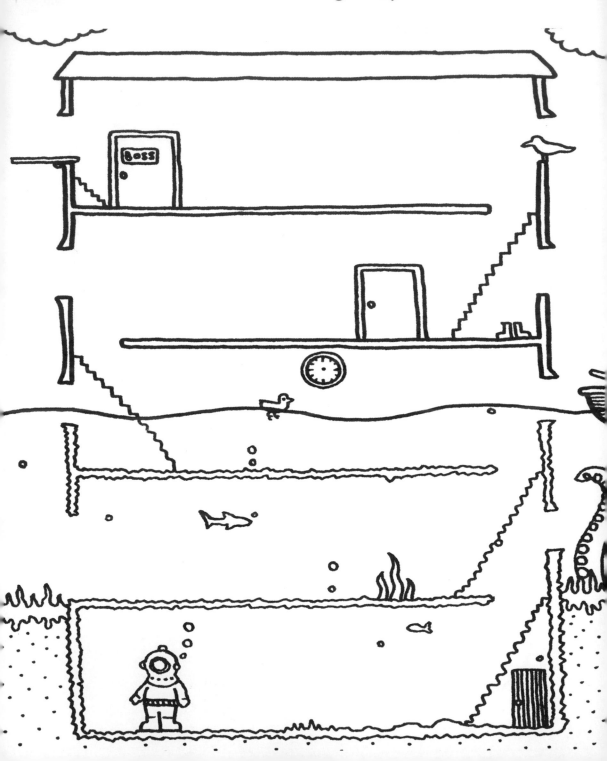

Make your big break bigger.

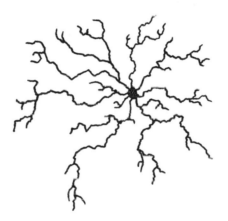

What is going on under the desks?

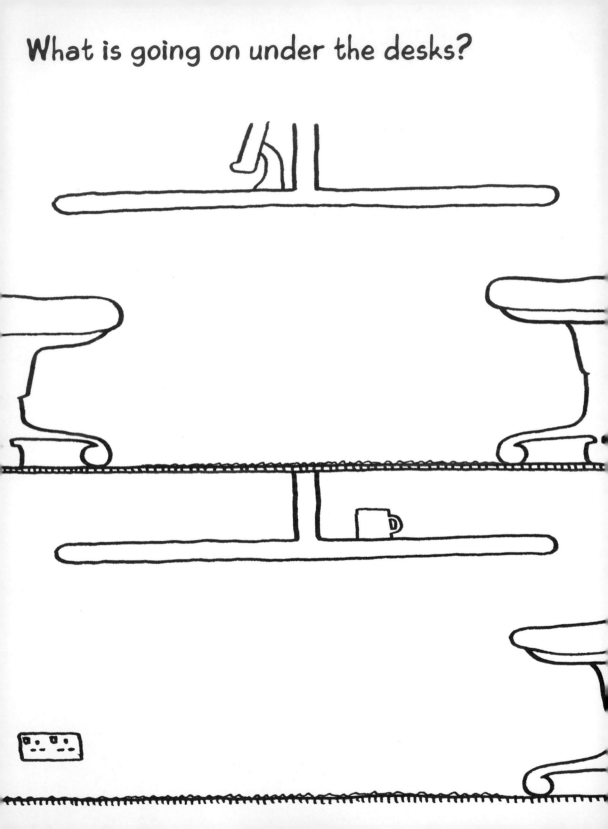

Rate your job stability.

FORTRESS ☐

SHACKLED ☐

PROTECTED ☐

COMFY CHAIR ☐

UNICYCLE ☐

TIGHTROPE ☐

CLINGING ON ☐

FINE LINE ☐

FREEFALL ☐

Arm the job hunters.

Sabotage the last page of Dave's flip chart.

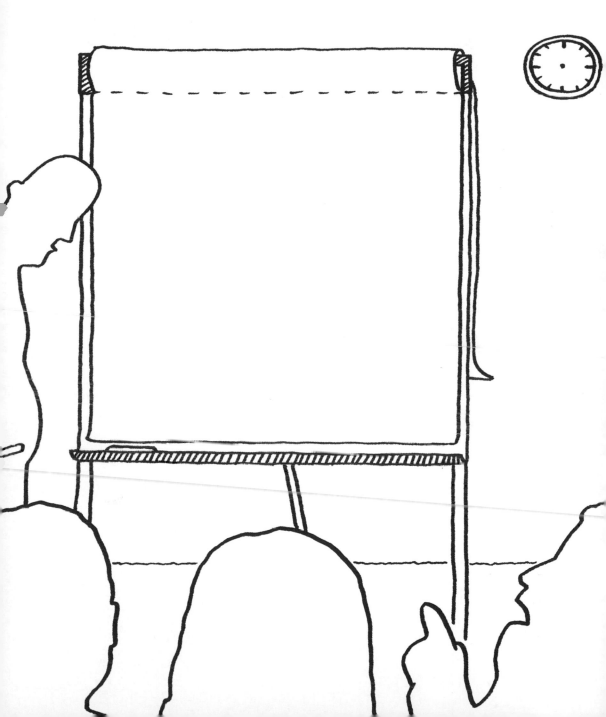

Relocate the office to a more suitable place.

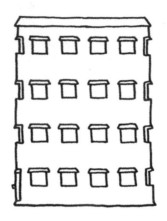

What remedy will you prescribe when you pull a sickie?

MY SYMPTOMS:

MY REMEDY:

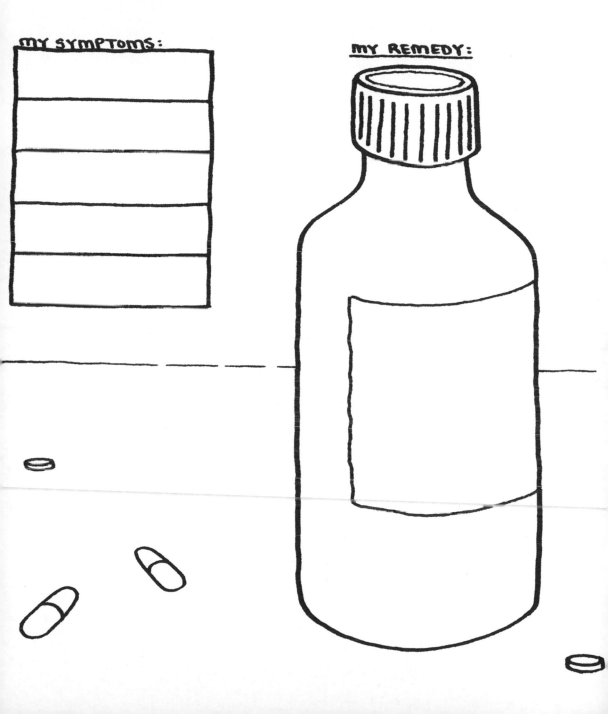

Put some leaky pens in your shirt pocket.

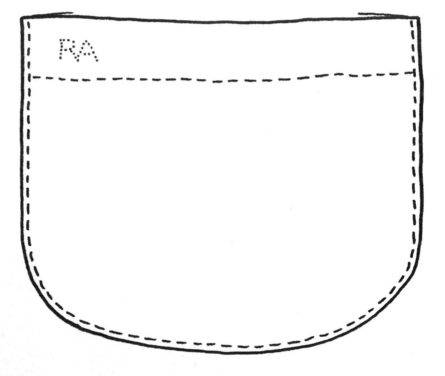

Dirty the competition.

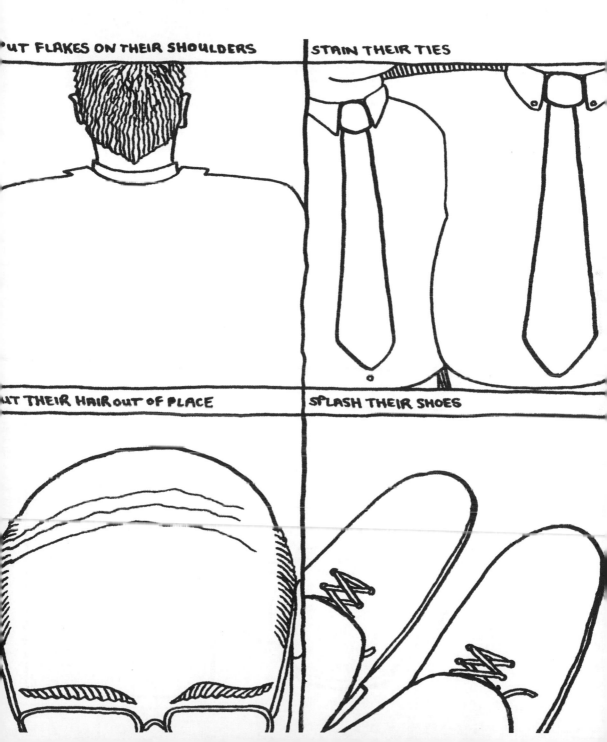

Summon the Tea Genie to grant you three cups.

1ST CUP

2ND CUP

3RD CUP

After-hours drinks with The Incredible Drunk.

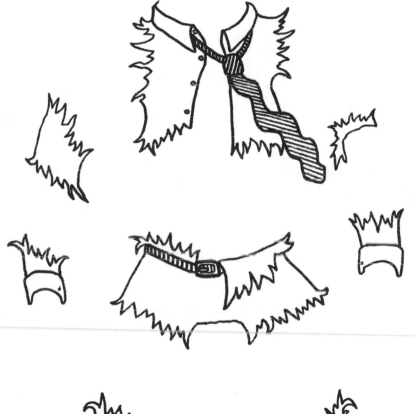

How will you get out of the red and into the black?

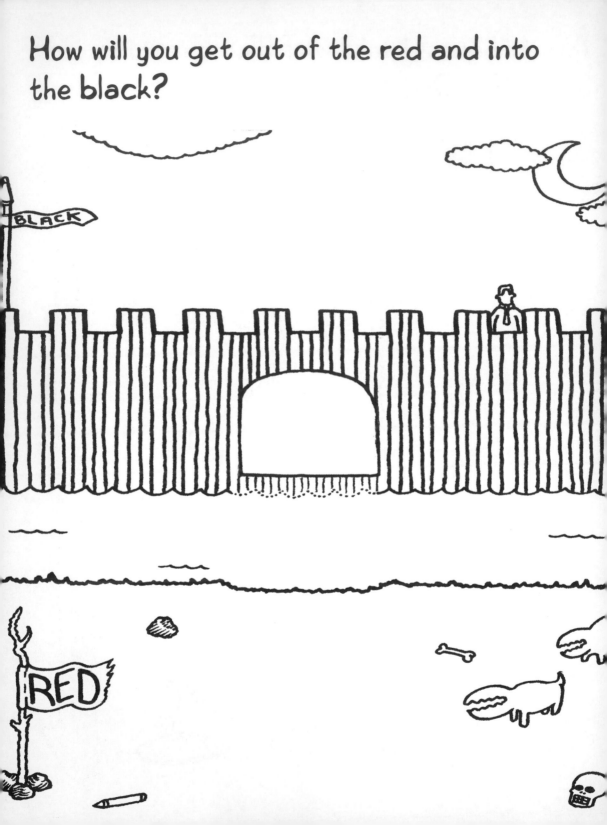

Identify your greed and bad deeds.

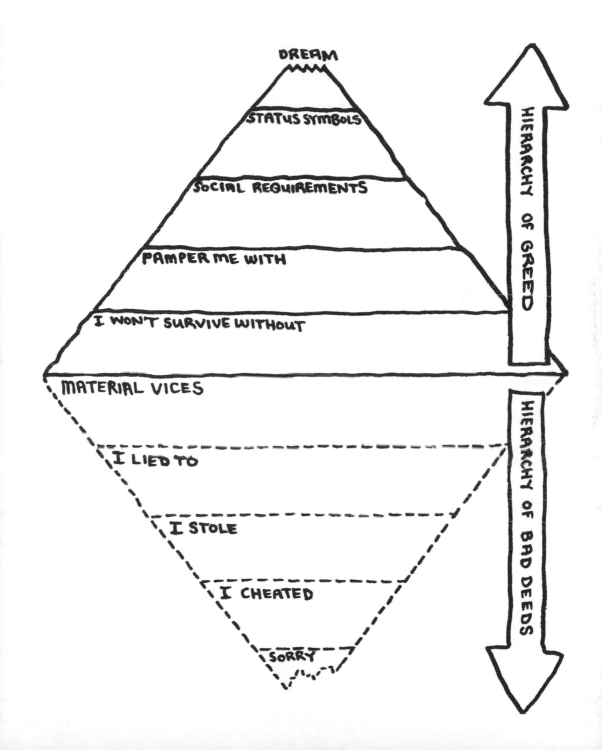

Brick up your office door.

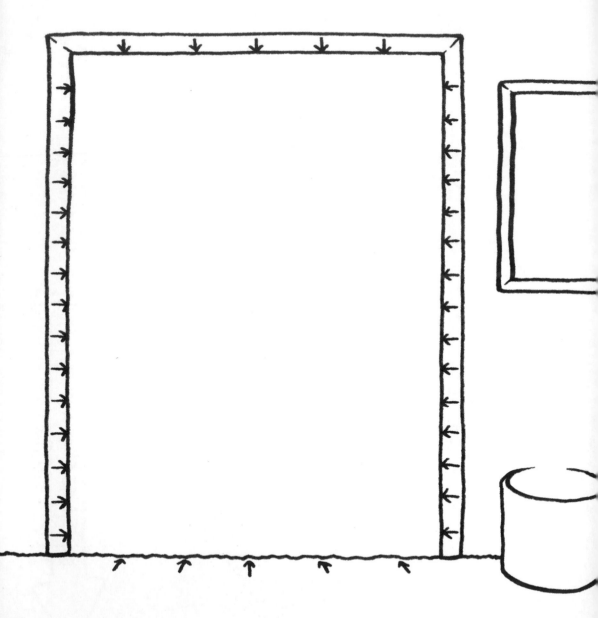

When do you finish work?

WHENEVER ☐

EARLY ☐

ON TIME ☑

LATE ☑

ON THE WAY HOME ☐

ON THE SOFA ☐

OVER DINNER ☐

SMALL HOURS ☐

NEVER ☐

Add some small print, sign on the dotted line and make sure you have a witness.

SIGNED:

CAN I GET A WITNESS?

Meet your targets.

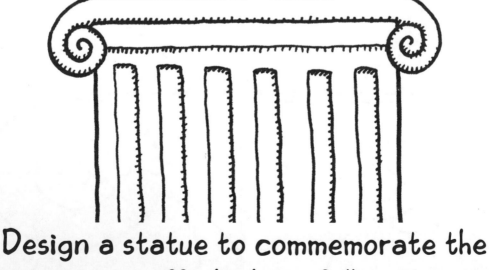

Design a statue to commemorate the
data entry staff who have fallen in action.

Secure the big contract.

How bright are your ideas?

Practise being patient with your computer.

1ST WAIT :	2ND WAIT :	3RD WAIT :
__hrs __mins __secs	__hrs __mins __secs	__hrs __mins __secs

Award yourself a medal for services beyond your call of duty.

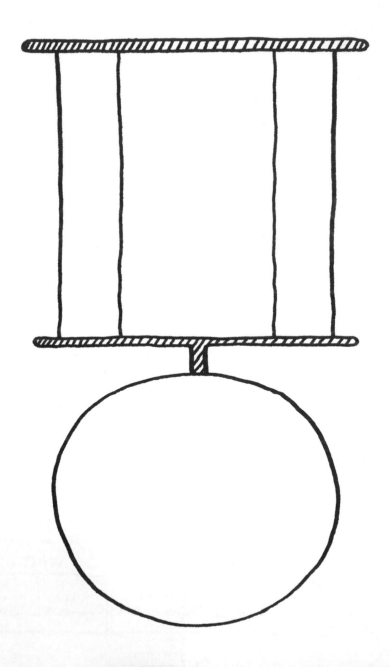

Design some new cufflinks for your colleagues.

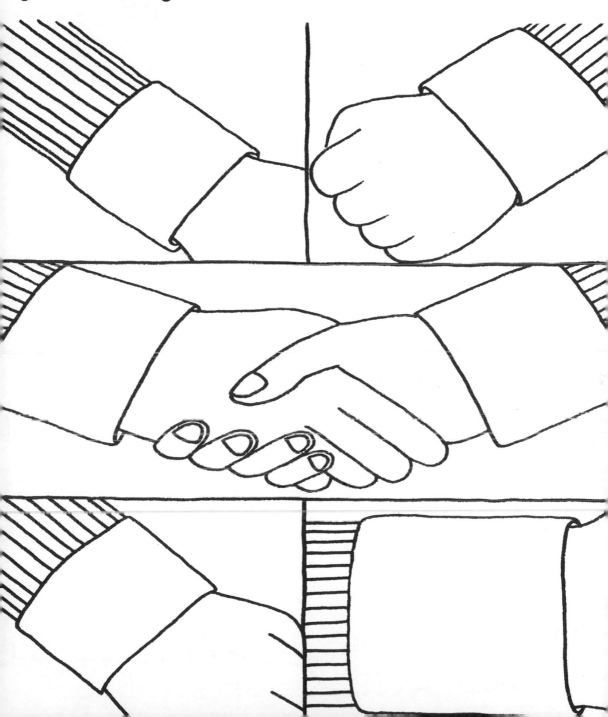

Bury yourself in paperwork and complete your gravestone.

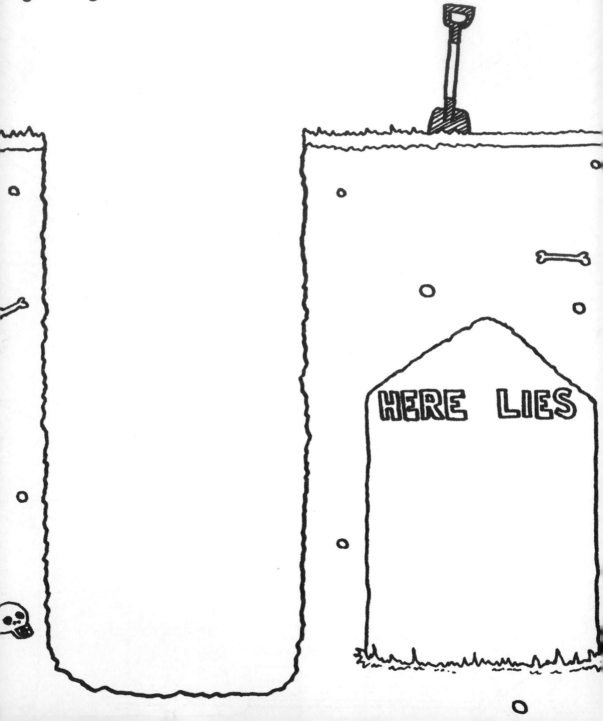

Help multitask with extra limbs.

decorate your workstation to feel more like home when you work weekends.

Complete the Boards of Directors' clubhouse photo.

the sales figures to give them a more attractive outline.

Draw the effects of different management styles on the staff faces.

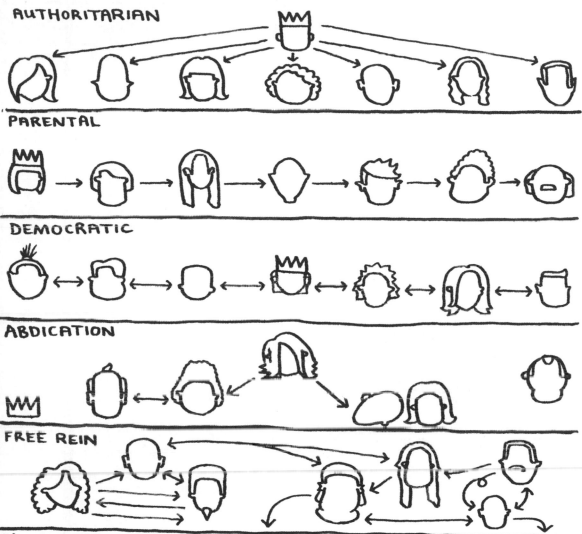

AUTHORITARIAN

PARENTAL

DEMOCRATIC

ABDICATION

FREE REIN

YOUR TURN

Will you pass your boss's lie detector test?

TRICKY QUESTIONS	YOUR RESPONSE		PASS?
DID YOU ARRIVE AT WORK ON TIME?			
♡			
HAVE YOU FINISHED THE ADMIN?			
♡			
HOW LONG DID YOU TAKE FOR LUNCH?			
♡			
DID YOU MEET YOUR TARGET?			
♡			
HAVE YOU SENT THAT EMAIL?			
♡			
WHERE ARE THE BISCUITS?			
♡			

What is the best way to throw the rule book?

Map the communication pathways for office gossip.

Don't shoot the messenger.

Find the weakest link in the chain of command.

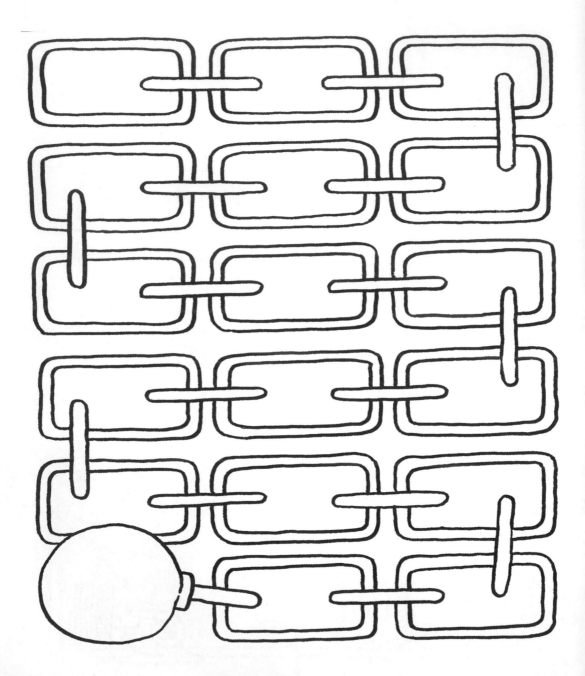

Board up the office and move on.

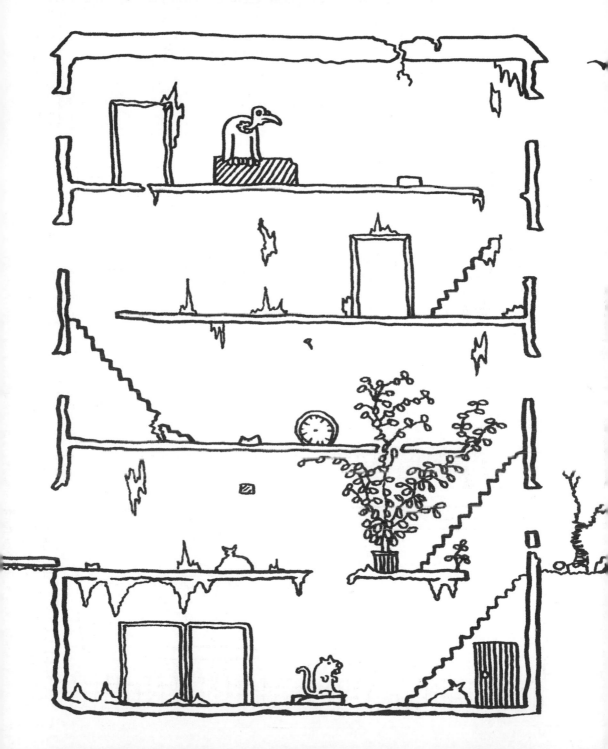

Certificate of Completion

Awarded to

_____

For outstanding contributions to the Bored @ Work Doodle Book

You have excelled in the following areas:

_____

_____

_____ and _____

These skills will serve you well.
Good Work.

SIGNED _____Rose Adders_____

DATE _____